Overcoming Anxiety and Fear

Brian Williams

Table of contents

Introduction

The word "anxiety" is used to describe a few different sorts of fear, most of which have to do with a threat or something going wrong in the future rather than right now.

Fear and worry can come on quickly and go away, but they can also linger for a very long period and keep you from moving forward. Sometimes they can take control of your life, making it difficult for you to eat, sleep, focus, travel, have fun, or even leave the house to go to work or school. This has an impact on your health and can prevent you from taking action that you need or want to.

Some people are so overcome by fear that they try to stay away from anything that can make them feel scared or nervous. Although there are several ways to do it, it might be challenging to break this cycle. You can develop coping mechanisms so that fear won't keep you from living. This will help you feel less scared.

What frightens you?

There are many things that frighten us. Some fears, such as a fear of burning, might actually keep you safe. Fear of failure can motivate you to work hard so that you won't fail, but if the feeling is too powerful, it can also prevent you from working hard.

Each person is different in what they are scared of and how they react to it. The first step in resolving issues with fear can be as simple as understanding what makes you afraid and why.

How do worry and dread feel?

Your body and thoughts move incredibly quickly when you're scared or extremely agitated. These are some of the potential outcomes:

- You find it difficult to focus on anything else.
- You feel dizzy.
- You feel frozen to the spot.
- You can't eat.
- You breathe quickly.
- Your muscles feel weak.
- You sweat a lot.
- Your stomach churns or your intestines feel loose.
- You get hot and cold sweats.
- Your mouth becomes dry.
- Your muscles become quite tense.

These events take place as a result of your body perceiving anxiety and preparing you for an emergency by increasing blood flow to the muscles, decreasing blood sugar levels, and enhancing your capacity to concentrate mentally.

In the long run, anxiety can cause some of the symptoms listed above as well as a more persistent feeling of fear. Additionally, anxiety can cause irritability, difficulty sleeping, headaches, difficulty focusing on work or making future plans, problems with sex, and self-confidence issues.

What exactly is a panic attack?

The symptoms stated under "What do fear and anxiety feel like?" are indications that you are having a panic attack, which is when you feel physically and mentally overcome by terror.
People who experience panic attacks report having trouble breathing and worrying that they may be suffering a heart attack or losing control of their bodies. If you need assistance with panic attacks, look at the "Support and information" section at the end of this guide.

How do phobias work?

A phobia is a strong aversion to a certain object, creature, setting, or circumstance. People who have phobias feel an intense need to stay away from whatever is causing them worry or terror.

What can I do to help myself?

If you can, confront your fear.
You might cease doing things you want to or need to do if you avoid frightening circumstances at all costs.
The opportunity to figure out how to control your concerns and lessen your anxiety is lost because you won't be able to determine whether the situation is always as horrible as you anticipate. If you fall into this cycle, your anxiety issues are likely to worsen. Making yourself vulnerable to your worries can help you get over this anxiety.

Knowing oneself

Try to gain more knowledge about your worry or fear. Keep a notebook or thought journal to document your anxiety and the events that follow.

A list of items that can be helpful when you are prone to feel scared or worried could be something you always have with you. This may be a powerful strategy for addressing the underlying assumptions that are the cause of your worry.

Chapter 1

Understanding anxiety disorder

Anxiety is a typical and frequently positive feeling. However, it could develop into a medical illness if a person experiences excessive amounts of worry regularly.

A group of mental health conditions known as anxiety disorders causes excessive trepidation, dread, apprehension, and concern.

In addition to generating physical symptoms, many illnesses change how a person behaves and processes emotions. While mild anxiety may be hazy and unpleasant, severe anxiety may significantly interfere with day-to-day activities.

In the US, 40 million people suffer from anxiety problems. It is the most prevalent subset of mental disorders in the nation. Only 36.9% of individuals with anxiety disorders obtain therapy, though.

Anxiety is "an emotion marked by feelings of tension, anxious thoughts, and bodily changes including elevated blood pressure," according to the American Psychological Association (APA).

It might be easier to recognize and get treatment for an anxiety problem if one knows the difference between typical anxious emotions and an anxiety disorder that needs medical attention.

Feelings of anxiety when one is exposed to potentially dangerous or disturbing stimuli are not only natural but also essential for life.

Since the beginning of time, humans have had physical alarms that enable them to take evasive action when predators or danger is around. These warnings manifest as elevated heart rate, perspiration, and enhanced sensitivity to the environment.

The "fight-or-flight" response, which is brought on by the adrenalin surge brought on by the threat, is a hormonal and chemical messenger that the brain produces. This makes people physically capable of fending off or escaping any potential dangers.

Running from bigger creatures and impending danger is a less urgent issue for many individuals than it would have been for early humans. These days, the main sources of anxiety are things like job, money, family life, health, and other important matters that need a person's attention but don't always call for the "fight-or-flight" response.

A natural echo of the original "fight-or-flight" response is the uneasy feeling that comes before a big life event or in the midst of a challenging scenario. It may still be necessary for survival; for instance, when crossing the street, someone who is afraid of being hit by a car may naturally look in both directions to stay safe.

Anxiety disorders

According to the APA, an individual with an anxiety disorder "has repeated intrusive thoughts or concerns." When anxiety becomes a problem, it can make it difficult to go about regular tasks.

Symptoms

Although many other diagnoses fall under the category of anxiety disorders, generalized anxiety disorder (GAD) symptoms frequently include the following:

- Feeling "on-edge" and a sense of restlessness
- Anxiety that won't go away
- Higher irritation
- Having trouble focusing

Issues with falling or staying asleep are examples of sleep issues.

Although these symptoms may be common in everyday life, GAD sufferers will experience them at excessive or chronic levels. GAD symptoms can range from vague, uncomfortable worry to intense anxiety that interferes with day-to-day activities.

Sometimes the intensity or duration of an anxious emotion is out of proportion to the stressor that first set it off. Additionally, physical symptoms like nausea and elevated blood pressure might appear. Through these reactions, anxiety becomes an anxiety disorder.

Types of anxiety

Anxiety disorders are divided into five primary kinds according to the Diagnostic and Statistical Manual of Mental Health Disorders, Fifth Edition (DSM-V).

Obsessive-compulsive disorder (OCD), post-traumatic stress disorder (PTSD), and acute stress disorder were all included as anxiety disorders in earlier DSM versions. These mental health issues are no longer classified as anxiety in the guideline, nevertheless.

The following diagnoses are now classified as anxiety disorders.

Generalized anxiety disorder: is a chronic condition characterized by persistent, excessive worry and concerns over unrelated people, things, and events in life. The most prevalent anxiety illness, GAD, leaves its sufferers unable to always pinpoint the source of their concern.

Panic disorder: Panic disorder is characterized by brief or unexpected spells of terrifying anxiety and concern. Shaking, disorientation, nausea, dizziness, and breathing difficulties might result from these attacks. Attacks of panic frequently start off mild and quickly worsen, culminating within ten minutes. A panic episode, however, might linger for several hours.

While they frequently follow terrifying events or periods of intense stress, panic disorders can sometimes strike suddenly. A person having a panic attack could mistake it for a serious sickness and alter their conduct drastically to prevent further episodes.

A specific phobia is an unfounded fear of or avoidance of a specific thing or circumstance.

Phobias differ from other anxiety disorders in that they have a known root cause.

A person who has a phobia may recognize a fear as unreasonable or severe, yet they are nonetheless unable to manage their worry when the trigger is present. A fear can be triggered by anything, from people or animals to commonplace items.

Agoraphobia: is the dread of, and avoidance of, places, occasions, or circumstances from which one could find it challenging to escape or where assistance would not be accessible should one get stuck. This disease is sometimes misunderstood as a fear of wide open spaces and the outdoors, but it is not as straightforward as that. A person who suffers from agoraphobia can be afraid to leave the house, use an elevator, or take public transportation.

Specific mutism: This is a type of anxiety that some kids go through where they can't communicate in specific settings or situations, like school, even though they may have good verbal communication abilities with known individuals. It might be a severe case of social phobia.

Social phobia: also known as social anxiety disorder, is the fear of being embarrassed in front of others or of receiving poor judgment from them in social circumstances.

Stage fright, a fear of intimacy, worry over rejection, and other emotions are all part of social anxiety disorder.

This illness can make people avoid social events and human contact to the point that it becomes exceedingly difficult to go about daily life.

Separation anxiety disorder is characterized by intense anxiety following separation from a person or environment that gives one a sense of security or safety. Panic symptoms can occasionally be brought on by separation.

Causes

Anxiety disorders have several root causes. Many might happen simultaneously, some could trigger others, and some could not even trigger an anxiety condition without another.

Environmental pressures, such as challenges at work, marital concerns, or family problems, are potential reasons. heredity, since individuals are more prone to develop an anxiety condition if they have relatives who do.

Medical variables such as a distinct disease's symptoms, a medication's side effects, the strain of an invasive procedure, or a lengthy recovery.

Brain chemistry, since many anxiety illnesses are described by psychologists as hormonal and electrical signal imbalances in the brain.

Withdrawal from a drug of abuse, whose effects may compound the symptoms of other potential causes

Anxiety is a normal feeling that is necessary for survival when a person finds themselves in a dangerous situation. It is not a medical issue.

When this response amplifies or is out of proportion to the stimulus that triggers it, an anxiety disorder develops. Anxiety disorders come in a variety of forms, such as social anxiety, phobias, and panic disorders.

Anxiety is a typical response to a wide range of occasions and circumstances in our life.
Anxiety is one of our body's inherent alarm systems that warns us of impending danger or other dangers and primes our bodies for combat or escape. This is referred to by scientists as the "fight, flight, or freeze" reaction.

An occasional bout of controllable anxiety might be beneficial. For instance, it could inspire you to accomplish a task at work or get ready for a test at school. Being human means that even joyful occasions like moving to a new house or achieving a significant milestone may cause worry.

Anxiety becomes an issue when it manifests unexpectedly, becomes overwhelming, or is uncontrollable. Mental problems like anxiety disorders can significantly affect your life.

Anxiety is one of our body's inherent alarm systems that warn us of impending danger or other dangers and primes our bodies for combat or escape. This is referred to by scientists as the "fight, flight, or freeze" reaction.

An occasional bout of controllable anxiety might be beneficial. For instance, it could inspire you to accomplish a task at work or get ready for a test at school. Being human means that even joyful occasions like moving to a new house or achieving a significant milestone may cause worry.

Anxiety becomes an issue when it manifests unexpectedly, becomes overwhelming, or is uncontrollable.

Mental problems like anxiety disorders can significantly affect your life. In order to prevent worry, some people choose not to go about their regular activities. They could go through a lot of unpleasant bodily feelings and health issues. Many people claim that while knowing that their worry is unfounded, they nonetheless feel "imprisoned" by their thoughts and emotions. Disorders of anxiety can be addressed. If anxiety is a problem in your life, it's crucial to get treatment.

Facts about typical anxiety

- Relates to a certain issue or scenario
- Lasts just as long as the issue or scenario
- Is proportionate to the issue or circumstance

When a person has a condition of anxiousness, they may feel a lot of irrational anxiety, such as worry over an event that is probably not going to happen.

Even after a situation or issue has been handled, anxiety might persist for a very long time.

It may seem hard to regulate or control anxiety.
They could stay away from situations or things that they think will make them feel anxious.

Here is an illustration of both typical anxiety and anxiety disorders. Many individuals experience some anxiety when they travel, which is a very natural emotion. However, if they need to travel for work, they won't have any trouble boarding an aircraft.

On the other hand, a person with an anxiety illness might be unable to go to the airport, even if it means risking their job.

How to distinguish between them

Being nervous or experiencing anxiety isn't necessarily a problem. You might almost think of it as a continuum or spectrum. It can occasionally aid in our preparation for events or assist in keeping us vigilant in risky circumstances. Furthermore, it's a typical response to stress. However, anxiety disorders are not a common response to stress.

In order for anything to be defined as an anxiety disorder as opposed to just being anxious, two factors often need to be present:

The anxiousness is either excessive for the circumstances or inappropriate for the person's age.

It makes it harder to carry out daily tasks normally.

Another typical discovery

Unusual and excessive anticipatory responses in the face of uncertainty are common among anxiety disorders.

Uncertainty is a part of everyone's life. However, a person who suffers from an anxiety illness could overestimate the uncertainty and possible outcomes in relation to the actual occurrence.

Anxiety disorder is different from "normal" anxiety.

Excessive and persistent worry that doesn't pass, even when there is no reason to be concerned or anxious, is what is meant by "abnormal" anxiety. When suffering from an anxiety condition, people frequently strive to avoid situations or items that aggravate their symptoms.

Real-world examples

It's normal to feel apprehensive or nervous before a test if you know you have a math exam later that day when you get up.

You could be experiencing heart palpitations, nausea, and frequent thoughts about the test and its potential outcomes. You'll probably feel more at ease and physically normal when the exam is finished.

It may be an indication of an anxiety disorder if you wake up one morning sure that something terrible will happen to a loved one, obsess about it the rest of the day, and then have intrusive thoughts about it the following day.

Excessive, difficult-to-control concern that lasts the majority of the day, most days, is a common feature of an anxiety disorder.

Significant physical manifestations of anxiety may also be present, such as:

headaches

fatigue

body aches

sleeping issues

digestive difficulties

Taking care of an anxiety problem

Be aware that if you have an anxiety problem, it is curable and controllable. It is worthwhile to receive an accurate diagnosis and subsequent treatment because you can feel better with the right care.

Chapter 2

Causes of Anxiety disorder

Anxiety disorders are unknown to have specific causes. The National Institute of Mental Health (NIMH)Trusted Source claims that a confluence of hereditary and environmental variables may be involved. As a potential reason, brain chemistry is also being researched. Your brain's regions in charge of controlling your fear reaction could be at play.

Anxiety disorders frequently co-occur with other mental health issues including drug addiction and depression. By using alcohol or other drugs, many people attempt to reduce the symptoms of anxiety. These medications only temporarily relieve symptoms. An anxiety problem can become worse with the use of alcohol, nicotine, caffeine, and other medications.

Current Investigation

There is a lot of study being done on the origins of anxiety disorders. According to experts, a variety of elements, including social stress and genetic factors, are at play.

Additionally, the hippocampus and amygdala of the brain are being investigated. Your brain's amygdala, a tiny region located deep inside, analyzes dangers. When there are indications of danger, it notifies the remainder of your brain. It could make someone feel scared or anxious. It appears to contribute to anxiety disorders if there is a specific phobia, such as a fear of cats, bees, or drowning.

Your hippocampus may also have an impact on how likely you are to acquire an anxiety condition. It is a part of your brain that is responsible for preserving memories of dangerous situations.

It seems to be less prevalent in those who were subjected to domestic violence as children or who have served in the military.

Causes

The following are some factors that might make you more likely to acquire an anxiety condition.

Stress

Everyone experiences stress, but too much or too much stress that isn't dealt with might raise your risk of having a persistent anxiety disorder.

In 2019, the authors of a study review trusted Source looked at several studies' findings that stress and anxiety have neurological connections. They concluded that neuronal characteristics in particular regions of the brain, such as the amygdala, which is involved in processing dangerous and frightening inputs, may aid in explaining how stress causes anxiety.

Genetic influences

You may be more likely to get an anxiety condition if someone in your family already has one. Although social and economic circumstances can have an impact, mounting research points to the possibility that hereditary characteristics may as well.

2019 research

Trusted Source investigated the relationships between anxiety and stress-related diseases and genetic traits. The authors came to the conclusion that having particular genetic traits may make you more prone to worry. These characteristics could be inherited.

Type of personality

Your likelihood of experiencing anxiety and anxiety disorders may be influenced by specific personality features.

Researchers studied 489 first-year university students for 6 years to determine how specific outlooks, such as a propensity for negative emotions, extraversion, and introversion, would increase the likelihood that they will experience anxiety and depression.

In addition, they discovered that major depressive disorder, agoraphobia, panic disorder, and generalized anxiety disorder (GAD) were more likely to develop over time in people who were hypercritical of themselves, had trouble accepting criticism, or had a lot of negative thoughts and feelings as young adults.

Additionally, those who scored highly on an introversion measure as opposed to an extroversion scale were more likely to suffer from agoraphobia.

Although they could serve as "vulnerability variables," the authors contend that they are likely a small portion of a much larger picture.

Trauma

Your chance of getting anxiety may rise if you have recently or in the past experienced a stressful incident, such as being abused or taking part in a battle. It may also occur if you have observed trauma or are close to someone who is experiencing trauma.

After a surprising or terrifying event, many people develop anxiety; this condition is known as acute distress disorder (ASD). Nevertheless, persistent symptoms can be an indication of post-traumatic stress disorder (PTSD). Although they might show up months or years after the occurrence, symptoms often begin within three months trusted Source.

They consist of:

flashbacks

awful dreams

feeling on edge all the time

inability to sleep

furious outbursts

avoiding locations or circumstances that can cause stress symptoms

ASD can occasionally develop into Trusted Source PTSD, however, this does not usually occur.

Racism

Even after accounting for hereditary characteristics, those who encounter racial discrimination have an increased chance of developing anxiety and anxiety disorders.

According to researchers who released a study in 2021, discrimination increases the likelihood of anxiety. The authors urged further education about the connection between racism, other types of discrimination, and social exclusion and how those factors might impact people's mental health.

Black individuals and Indigenous People of Color in the United States are at risk of traumatic stress disorder based on race, according to Mental Health America (MHA) (RBTS).

If you have an "emotionally traumatic, abrupt, and uncontrollable racist encounter," RBTS may have an impact on you. The symptoms can have an impact on a larger group and are comparable to those of PTSD. MHA notes that RBTS is not a mental illness but rather a mental damage, in contrast to PTSD.

Discover more here on how to identify and handle racial trauma.

Sex

According to studies, women are more likely than men to experience anxiety and suffer the onset of an anxiety disorder, however this may vary somewhat depending on the disorder.

The following rates seem to be greater in females than in males:

Anxiety disorder

Agoraphobia

Generalized anxiety disorder

Phobias

Separation anxiety

Post-traumatic stress disorder (PTSD)

However, obsessive-compulsive disorder (OCD) and social anxiety disorder (SAD) may affect both men and women equally (OCD). The two anxiety disorders that afflict men most frequently are OCD and SAD.

The cause is probably a mix of biological and social or cultural variables, but more research is needed to determine how each contributes specifically, according to the experts.

Anxiety can also be brought on by worries about sexual performance.

Gender dysphoria

Those who have gender dysphoria do not identify with the gender that was given to them at birth.

This can confuse and worry, but it can also raise your risk of confrontation with others, especially if they have inflexible ideas about the roles that men and women should play in society.

Statistics from a Reliable Source indicate that many individuals with gender dysphoria run the risk of:

- Anxiety disorders and tension
- Depression
- Considering suicide
- Usage of drugs
- Health reasons

A person's health may influence stress in several ways, including:

Experiences with mental and physical health in the past and present

Having a persistent condition that makes daily life difficult

Having a sickness with extremely difficult symptoms, like palpitations

Having a medical condition, such as a hormone imbalance, where anxiety is a symptom

These won't always result in anxiety disorders.

Happenings in life

According to the American Institute of Stress, life experiences, including trauma, might raise your risk of stress and anxiety.

Examples include:

losing a loved one

divorce or separation

spending time in the criminal justice system

injury or illness

financial pressures or a loss of employment

major changes, such as moving into a new house or getting married

A person can experience these events without developing an anxiety disorder, although some may do so.

What causes anxiety attacks?

Triggers for anxiety vary widely between individuals. Different anxiety disorders will also have different triggers. Things that can cause feelings of anxiety in some people to include:

- Health issues

- The use of some substances, such as drugs or caffeine
- Lifestyle factors, such as financial worries
- Either being alone or being with a lot of people
- Conflict
- Reminders of past trauma

Risk factors

Many factors can increase the severity of anxiety symptoms. Some may be specific to an anxiety disorder, but risk factors overall can include the following, according to the NIMHTrusted Source:

Personality traits, such as shyness in childhood

Experience of traumatic events

A family history of mental health challenges

Some physical conditions, such as a thyroid disorder

Risk elements

The degree of anxiety symptoms can be impacted by a variety of circumstances. According to the NIMHTrusted Source, some risk factors may be exclusive to an anxiety disorder, but overall they might include the following:

Personality traits like childhood shyness

Previous exposure to terrible situations

A history of mental health issues in the family

Some health ailments, including a thyroid issue

Chapter 3

Fear

Fear is a natural, strong, and common human emotion. Both a widespread physiological reaction and a strong personal emotional reaction are involved. Whether the threat is psychological or physical, fear serves as a warning when danger is present.

Worry may come from both genuine and imagined hazards. Real threats can sometimes be the source of fear. Some mental health illnesses, such as panic disorder, social anxiety disorder, phobias, and post-traumatic stress disorder, can also show symptoms of fear (PTSD).

Biochemical and emotional responses to a perceived danger make up the two main components of fear.

Biochemical Reaction

Fear is a healthy feeling and a form of survival. When we encounter a threat, our bodies react in particular ways.

Fear causes us to physically respond by sweating profusely, speeding up our hearts, and being more alert due to high adrenaline levels.

Your body prepares for either fighting or flight with this physiological reaction, which is often referred to as the "fight or flight" response. This metabolic process is probably a result of evolution. It is a natural reaction that is essential to our existence.

Emotional reaction

On the other hand, each person's reaction to fear is very unique. Feeling fear in some conditions, such as when you watch scary movies, may be perceived as enjoyable because it triggers some of the same chemical processes in our brains that good emotions like happiness and enthusiasm do.

Signs of Fear

Fear frequently causes both physical and emotional side effects. While everyone experiences fear differently, the following are some typical indicators and symptoms:

Chest pain

Chills

mouth ache

Nausea

a quick heartbeat

breathing difficulty

Sweating

Trembling

uneasy stomach

People may suffer psychological symptoms such as feeling overwhelmed, disturbed, out of control, or a sensation of imminent death in addition to the physical signs and symptoms of terror.

Identifying Fear

If your emotions of dread are extreme and persistent, speak with your doctor. In order to make sure that your worry and dread are not caused by an underlying medical problem, your doctor may undertake a physical examination and blood testing.

Your doctor will also inquire about your symptoms, including their duration, severity, and circumstances that often bring them on. Your doctor may determine that you have an anxiety condition such as a phobia based on your symptoms.

Phobias

The tendency to experience the dread of fear can be one symptom of anxiety disorders.

Those who suffer from anxiety disorders may become worried that they will feel terror, but most people typically only feel fear when it is associated with a scary or dangerous circumstance. They actively try to avoid their fear reactions because they see them as bad.

An abnormal fear reaction is called a phobia.
The thing or circumstance that is causing the dread is not actually dangerous. Even if you are aware that the worry is unwarranted, you are unable to stop yourself. As the dread of terror reaction sets in, the fear has a tendency to get worse with time.

Reasons for Fear

Fear is a very intricate emotion. Some anxieties may be brought on by traumatic events or experiences, while others may be a dread of something completely different, like losing control. Other phobias, such as a fear of heights because they make you feel lightheaded and queasy, may arise as a result of physical symptoms.

Common things that make people dread include:

certain things or circumstances (spiders, snakes, heights, flying, etc)

Future activities

Imaginary things

actual environmental risks

The unknown

Due to their role in survival, some anxieties are often natural and may have evolved. Others are acquired and linked to associations or upsetting events.

Types of fear

Fear is a characteristic of several distinct forms of anxiety disorders, such as:

Agoraphobia

Disorder of generalized anxiety

Panic attack

Post-traumatic stress disorder (PTSD)

Separation anxiety disorder

Social anxiety disorder

Specific phobia

Combating Fear

Familiarity, which results from repeated exposure to identical circumstances, can significantly lessen both the terror response. Some phobia treatments use this strategy as its foundation since it works to gradually reduce the fear reaction by making it feel familiar.

Treatments for phobias that are based on the psychology of fear frequently include methods like flooding and systematic desensitization. Both methods diminish fear by influencing your body's physiological and psychological reactions.

Desensitization in a systematic way

You are gradually guided through a succession of exposure situations with systematic desensitization. For instance, if you're afraid of snakes, your therapist and you might spend the first session discussing snakes.

Your therapist would guide you gradually over the course of several sessions while you practiced touching a real snake, playing with toy snakes, and looking at photographs of snakes. This is typically done in conjunction with learning and using fresh coping mechanisms to control the terror reaction.

Flooding

This kind of exposure strategy has the potential to be quite effective. Flooding on the grounds that you must unlearn your phobia because it is a taught behavior. In a safe, controlled atmosphere, you are exposed to a great deal of the dreaded object or circumstance when you flood, and this exposure lasts for a long time until the fear passes. For instance, even if you're frightened of flying, you'd still board a plane.

Managing Fear

You can also take actions to assist you deal with fear in daily life. These methods concentrate on controlling the negative behavioral, emotional, and bodily impacts of fear. Among the things you can accomplish are:

Obtain social assistance.

You can better control your feelings of dread by surrounding yourself with encouraging people.

Engage in mindfulness.

Even if you can't always control your emotions, mindfulness can help you control them and replace unhelpful thoughts with constructive ones.

Use stress-reduction methods including progressive muscle relaxation, visualization, and deep breathing.

Take good care of yourself.

Eat healthily, exercise frequently, and get enough sleep each night.

Chapter 4

Meditation

Meditation is a quick and easy method for reducing stress.

Stress from the day can be eliminated through meditation, which also brings inner calm.

Try meditation if stress is causing you to feel tense, worried, or anxious. Even a brief period of meditation might help you regain your composure and inner serenity.

Meditation is accessible to everyone. It is easy and reasonably priced. Additionally, no special tools are needed.

Additionally, you can meditate anywhere you are, including when taking a walk, taking the bus, waiting for a doctor, or even in the middle of a challenging work meeting.

Understanding meditation

The practice of meditation dates back thousands of years. The initial purpose of meditation was to aid in a deeper comprehension of life's mystical and sacred forces. Nowadays, meditation is frequently used to relieve and reduce stress.

One form of supplementary medicine for the mind and body is meditation. Deep relaxation and mental calmness are two effects of meditation.

You concentrate during meditation and get rid of the constant stream of disorganized ideas that could be stressing you out. The approach may lead to improved mental and emotional health.

Advantages of meditation

You may improve both your physical and emotional health by practicing meditation, which can help you feel quiet, peaceful, and in balance.

By concentrating your attention on something peaceful, you can also utilize it to calm and manage stress. You can learn to keep your focus and maintain inner serenity by practicing meditation.
And once your meditation session is over, these advantages continue to exist. By shifting your attention to something peaceful, you can also utilize it to calm and manage stress.

You can learn to keep your focus and maintain inner serenity by practicing meditation.

Additionally, meditation may aid in the management of certain medical disorders' symptoms.

When you meditate, you might be able to get rid of the information overload that accumulates throughout the day and adds to your tension.

The advantages of meditation for both physical and emotional well-being can be:

Gaining fresh insight into difficult circumstances

Acquiring techniques for stress management

Increasing awareness of oneself

Keeping the present in mind

Lowering negative feelings

Increasing creativity and imagination

Increasing tolerance and patience

Lowering the heart rate at rest

Lowering the blood pressure at rest

Enhancing the caliber of sleep

Meditating while unwell

If you have a medical problem, especially one that could be made worse by stress, meditation may also be helpful.

Although a growing body of scientific evidence points to the health benefits of meditation, some academics think it is still too early to draw any firm judgments about such benefits.

In light of this, some study indicates that meditation may assist individuals in reducing the symptoms of ailments like:

Anxiety

Asthma

Cancer

Enduring pain

Depression

Heart condition

Elevated blood pressure

Rheumatoid bowel syndrome

Issues with sleep

Headaches with tension

If you suffer from any of these ailments or other health issues, be sure to discuss the benefits and drawbacks of meditation with your doctor. In certain extremely rare situations, meditation may make symptoms related to particular mental health issues worse.

Traditional medical care cannot be substituted with meditation. However, it might be a helpful supplement to your current therapy.

Types of meditation

The term "meditation" is used to describe a variety of techniques for achieving a calm state of being. The components of meditation can be found in many different relaxation and meditation techniques. The pursuit of inner serenity is a common objective for all.

Some techniques for meditation include:

A meditation class.

With this type of meditation, also known as guided imagery or visualization, you create mental pictures of settings or circumstances that you find soothing.

You make an effort to engage all of your senses, including smells, sights, sounds, and textures. An instructor or advisor may lead you through this procedure.

Mantra-based meditation

To stop distracting thoughts, you silently repeat a relaxing term, idea, or phrase throughout this sort of meditation.

Consciousness training

Being attentive, or having a greater awareness and acceptance of existing in the present moment, is the foundation of this style of meditation.

During mindfulness meditation, your conscious awareness is widened. During meditation, you pay attention to the sensations you are having, including how your breath is moving. Your ideas and feelings are visible. But do not pass judgment; let them go.

Components of meditation

To aid with meditation, many techniques may have a variety of aspects. These may change based on whose advice you heed or who is instructing a class. The following are some of the most typical aspects of meditation:

Focused attentiveness

One of the most crucial aspects of meditation is generally being able to focus your mind.

You may free your mind from the numerous distractions that lead to stress and worry by focusing your attention.

Calm breathing: This method calls for slow, even breathing that expands your lungs by employing your diaphragm muscle. The idea is to breathe more slowly, inhale more oxygen, and breathe more efficiently by using fewer shoulder, neck, and upper chest muscles.

A calm environment.

If you're a beginner, it could be simpler to meditate if you're in a place with few distractions, such as one without television, radio, or telephones.

As you develop your meditation skills, you could be able to meditate anywhere, especially in high-stress situations when it will be most beneficial for you, like a traffic jam, a difficult work meeting, or a long grocery line.

A relaxed position. Whether you're seated, lying down, walking, or engaged in another activity, you can meditate. Just make an effort to be at ease so that you can benefit the most from your meditation. Maintain a straight spine while you are meditating.

Open mindset

Allow yourself to think without filtering them.

Simple techniques for meditating

Avoid letting the idea of meditating "properly" increase your anxiety. You can choose to go to specialized meditation facilities or classes for groups guided by qualified teachers. However, it is equally simple to meditate on your own. Or you could discover apps to utilize.

Additionally, you can make meditation as formal or informal as you wish, depending on your preferences and environment.

Some individuals incorporate meditation into their everyday schedule. For instance, they might spend an hour meditating at the beginning and end of each day. But all you truly need is a short period of focused meditation time.

Here are some techniques for independent meditation that you can use whenever you like:

Take a long breath.

Since breathing is a natural process, this technique is suitable for beginners.

Concentrate solely on your breathing. As you breathe in and out through your nostrils, pay close attention to how you're feeling and hearing. Slowly and deeply inhale. When your thoughts stray, gently bring them back to your breathing.

Do a body scan.

When utilizing this method, pay close attention to various body sections.

Recognize the many sensations you are experiencing in your body, such as pain, tension, warmth, or relaxation.

Exercise your breathing while scanning your body, and visualize breathing heat or relaxation into and out of various bodily areas.

Say a mantra aloud.

You can come up with your own mantra, whether it be spiritual or not. The Jesus Prayer in the Christian tradition, the holy name of God in Judaism, or the om mantra of Hinduism, Buddhism, and other Eastern religions are examples of religious mantras.

Stroll while doing some meditation.

A productive and beneficial technique to unwind is to combine meditation with a walk. This method can be applied anyplace you're strolling, including a serene forest, a metropolitan sidewalk, or a shopping center.

To concentrate on each movement of your legs or feet when using this technique, slow down your walking speed. Don't concentrate on a specific location. Focus on your legs and feet, lifting each one, pushing each leg forward, and setting each foot down while mentally repeating action phrases like "lifting," "moving," and "putting." Keep your attention on the sights, sounds, and smells in the area.

Make time for prayer.

The most well-known and frequently used form of meditation is prayer. In most religious traditions, there are both spoken and written prayers.

You have the option of saying your prayers out loud or reading others'.

Look for examples in the self-help section of your neighborhood bookshop. Consult your pastor, priest, rabbi, or other spiritual authority about available resources.

Read and think.

Many people claim that reading poems or sacred texts and giving themselves some time to think about their meaning in silence has positive effects.

You can also listen to any calming or motivating music, spoken word, or spiritual music. You might want to journal your reflections or talk about them with a close friend or spiritual guide.

Developing your meditative abilities

Don't criticize your meditation abilities because doing so could make you more stressed. It takes practice to meditate.

Remember, for instance, that no matter how long you've been practicing meditation, it's normal for your mind to wander during that time. When you're using meditation to relax your mind and it wanders, carefully bring it back to the sensation, action, or item you're concentrating on.

Try different meditation techniques to see which ones suit you the best and which ones you love. To suit your current demands, adjust your meditation. There is no right or wrong method to meditate, so keep that in mind. What is important is that practicing meditation makes you feel less stressed and more relaxed overall.

www.ingramcontent.com/pod-product-compliance
Lightning Source LLC
LaVergne TN
LVHW052109160826
845678LV00015B/3446

* 9 7 9 8 8 4 4 4 6 1 4 9 1 *